Help, I've Fallen And Need a Good Laugh!

Help, I've Fallen & Need A Good Laugh!

John Grogan

Evergreen
PRESS

ISBN 1-58169-160-2
For Worldwide Distribution
Printed in the U.S.A.

Evergreen Press
P.O. Box 191540
Mobile, AL 36619

Dedication

Dedicated to my Father who gave me a life that will
never pass away; His Son who showed me a book
that will get me home, and a Friend that sticks
closer than a brother.

Acknowledgements

My deep appreciation to you, Brian, for all your input and guidance. To you, Kathy, for the long hours of editing and arranging. And to you Jeff, always eager to help. And all of you whose names I do not know, for insuring that the books get out the door and onto the shelves. Thank you all; I couldn't do it without you.

Introduction

Bob Hope said, "Humor is a very serious business." What he meant was that making something funny for a wide audience is difficult work. But to connect something that is funny to a serious point is every bit as challenging and much more rewarding. The Bible is replete with how laughter contributes to a happy countenance.

Humor has suffered a setback however. ABC for example, has plans to air a new show called "Trading Moms" based on the program "Wife Swap" now airing in the U.K. ABC has been seduced and cannot resist the lure of the buck. They are willing to desecrate not only good, clean humour, but also the institution of marriage, parenthood, and family.

In this time of pervasive perversion, humor can still have the pristine quality that the T.V. comedy shows had in the 50s and 60s. Funny is funny. The new avant-garde humour that is based on double entendre has gone beyond offensive.

This book is an attempt to put a finger in the dike. The objective of this book is not solely to make you laugh just for the sake of a laugh —although there is a growing body of clinical evidence, which suggests laughter reduces stress leading to all kinds of ailments, including heart attacks.

Years ago Norm Cousins, at that time the editor of *Saturday Review* magazine, was struck down with an illness that confounded the doctors. Unable to get an accurate diagnose, Cousins took matters into his own hands. He ordered his aides to bring him several old Max Senate movies, and those starring Charlie Chaplin, Buster Keaton, and Harold Lloyd among others. Cousins states that he literally laughed himself back to good health.

This book is different. I not only want to give you, the reader, the gift of laughter, but medicine for the soul. Even if you're one of those unfortunate souls that were born unlucky and suffered a relapse, the humor "Dr. Grogan" serves up in this little tome will help the medicine go down. Laughter makes for a happy and healthy heart, and helps us get through this old world with fewer bruises and scrapes.

God invented laughter—enjoy it!

Not As We Thought...

After a hard two weeks of winter weather, a couple from the North decided to take a short break and head for the sunny beaches of southern Florida. The husband departed on a Monday, to be followed two days later by his wife. She was busy with final details in a real estate transaction.

After a flight cancellation and a failed appeal to higher management, he arrived at their hotel a day late. Florida was having unseasonably hot weather, so, he decided to send a quick e-mail giving his wife a heads-up.

Unfortunately he made an error in the address and his message arrived at the home of an elderly preacher's wife whose husband had just passed away. When the poor, dear widow opened the e-mail, she took one look at the message, shrieked, and fainted dead away.

The message on the screen read:
Dearest wife,
Departed yesterday as you know. Just got checked in. Some confusion at the gate. Appeal was denied. Received confirmation of your arrival tomorrow.

Your loving husband...
P.S. Things are not as we thought. You're going to be surprised at how hot it is down here."

Misunderstood

There were several people waiting for the airport shuttle when a one-eyed dog walked by. One of them said, "Look at that dog with one eye!" Five people covered one eye with their hand and watched the dog with the other as it passed by.

Many times we react in a knee-jerk fashion. We simply respond without thinking, which can lead to serious consequences if tensions are running high or we're stressed out by the pressures of life. Before we wind up leaving footprints on our tongue, we might want to pause and select. Pause long enough to select a proper response. In many cases the proper response will be...silence.

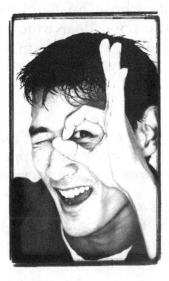

What Then?

After weighing himself, a man's wife was reading the little card bearing his fortune. "It says here that you are a born leader; that you have great long range vision; that you are a man of character, and will go far in life...it's got your weight wrong too!"

We don't have to read tea leaves or break open fortune cookies to tell our own future. We merely have to ask ourselves a simple two-word question: What then? For example: "I want to graduate from school and get a good job." What then? "Get married probably, settle down." What then? "Retire when I hit fifty-five." What then? "Well...I suppose die!" What then? A thousand years from now we'll all be somewhere!

Rain or Shine

They tell the story of a small prairie farm community that hadn't had rain in over a year. The ground looked like cracked leather. One day they decided to call a meeting at the church and pray for rain. That evening every person in town showed up, but a ten-year-old boy was the only one to bring an umbrella.

Hebrews 11:6 says we must come in faith believing. Part of the problem is that we're a pop tart society, an instant gratification nation. "By perseverance," the great English Baptist preacher, Charles Spurgeon once said, "the snail reached the Ark."

Dead or Alive?

This notice was posted on a church bulletin board by a lonely pastor: The church regrets to announce that it has come to our attention that people are dying in the pews and failing to fall down. This practice must stop as it becomes impossible to distinguish between death and normal movement of the saints. In the future any brother or sister found dead in an upright position will be dropped from the church register.

God doesn't call us into the church to sit down. We have to move from maintenance to mission, from the pews to purpose. With regard to the great commission, we are either fishing or merely maintaining an aquarium.

Stranger Than Fiction

A man approached a sales clerk in a bookstore and asked, "Have you a book titled *Man, the Master of Woman*?' The salesgirl, pointing her finger said, "The fiction department is over there, sir."

Some men still have a finely tuned sixteenth century mind.

Do It Now!

A man met his friend on the street and in the course of conversation inquired about the man's son who was in college. "What's he going to be when he gets out of school?" he asked. His friend thought for a moment and then said, "Forty-two, I think."

Some people are always getting ready to begin to commence to get started perhaps maybe tomorrow. Always getting ready to live but never really living! To always live in the future is fantasy. To reside in the past is sad. But to fail to seize today is tragic. Yesterday's a cancelled check; tomorrow's a promissory note; only today is legal tender.

"This is the day the Lord hath made, I will rejoice in it and be glad" (Psalm 118:24).

Grouchy

A woman asked her friend if she ever woke up grouchy in the morning. "No," the friend replied, "I just let him sleep in."

I had a friend who was like this...the room brightened up when he walked out of it!

One of the greatest causes of discontent is ingratitude. One of the greatest cures for this malady is to compose a list of all that we have to be grateful for. If you're stymied as to where to begin, start with knowing the Creator of the universe.

Simplicity

A seven-year-old girl was asked what she thought Noah's wife's name was. With full confidence and no hesitation the little girl answered, Joan of Arc.

Sometimes we make things so convoluted that people walk away confused. The story of salvation and what Jesus Christ did for us is a very simple message.

9

Trumped!

An elderly dowager was taking her friend for a ride in her new Rolls Royce. With a tone of condescension, she asked her friend if she'd ever ridden in a Rolls before. The friend replied demurely, "Not in the front seat."

Our society has elevated to hero status the person skilled in the "put down." This skill has been raised to an art form by the television sitcom. In real life, the one who trumps doesn't really win, and the one trumped never forgets.

Words can be used as weapons or as tools. What we say probably affects more people than any other action we take. We are either a wrecking ball or a builder.

Who's the Boss?

A man and his wife attended a lecture. The speaker was one of those insufferable stuffed suits with a finely developed 16th century mind. He droned on *ad nauseam* about many things and how they should be done. Included in this sermonizing was how the husband should reign with absolute sovereignty, brooking no backchat from spouse or scions alike.

The husband loved it; his wife, however, fumed as she listened to this Neanderthal babble on. After they left the lecture hall that evening, the husband felt imbued with new power.

When they arrived home the wife got out of the car and followed her husband silently into the house. Once inside, the husband told his wife to stop where she was. "Just stand right there," he said in a militaristic tone. "I've been thinking about what the speaker said tonight and I want you to know that from now on that's the way it's going to be around here. You got it?"

Having said that, he didn't see her for two weeks. After two weeks he could begin to see her just a little bit out of one eye.

A Spanish proverb says that in the land of the

blind the one eyed man rules. The eye is the symbol of light. In response to a question posed by a reporter, "Would you rather have sight than anything else?" the great blind lecturer, Helen Keller, responded, "I'd rather walk in the dark with a friend than be alone in the light."

The heart knows its own bitter sorrows and a stranger does not share its joy. We should never forget in the light what we learned in the darkness.

Winners and Losers

While at work a woman discovered that she had won several million dollars in the state lottery. She called home and told her husband the good news and said, "Pack for a trip!" The husband asked if he should pack for warm climes or cool climes. "It doesn't matter," she replied, "Just be gone by the time I get home!"

Life isn't always easy. Sometimes we're going to have tough days. Promising careers have been lost over one bad day; something said that couldn't be retrieved. Some people never miss an opportunity to miss an opportunity. We should never reach conclusions in the middle of the matter.

Shhhh!

Three men were talking about the particular problems they dealt with in life—the dragons they fought every day. The first man confessed that his problem was lying. "Everyone thinks so highly of me," he said, "if they only knew."

The second man said, "With me it's lust of the eyes. And people think I'm so holy."

Turning to the third man they asked what his besetting sin was. "Gossip" the man replied.

Choose your confidants carefully!

Wanderers

A bush pilot was flying over an island one day when he noticed a man waving frantically from the shore. Gently landing his pontoon equipped plane, he taxied to an inlet. As the man on the island was recounting to the pilot how he had come to be stranded on the island for five years, the pilot noticed three rather substantial structures.

"What do you need with three structures?" the pilot asked out of curiosity.

"Well" the man said, "the one on the left is my house. The one on the right is my church. The one in the center is where I used to go to church."

Many people wander from church to church when God never called them out. Proverbs 27:8

Keep On...

A friend of mine said, "I kept going to church trying to find the answer...and kept going to church trying to find the answer! Finally I realized the answer was to keep going to church!"

Like tennis, golf, or an exercise program, we get into it and then it gets into us! God works most closely through His Bride, the Church.

Heads Up

The softest pillow is a clear conscience.

Who's the Boss?

A man died and found himself facing the pearly gates. He noticed there were two lines of men trying to get into heaven. The one line stretched for miles, the other line only had one man standing in it. He approached the man standing alone in his line and asked who's standing in the long line. The man replied that it's made up of all the men who were bossed by their wives while on earth. "Why are you standing in this line by yourself?" he asked of the man. "I don't know," the man replied, "my wife told me to stand here."

Sometimes when God says, "Stand silent and know that I am God," we find that so intolerably difficult. Our society's attitude of, "If it is to be, it is up to me," says, "Don't just stand there, do something!" But God says, "Apart from Me you can do nothing."

Catch Me If You Can!

There was a young boy watching the postmaster put up a picture of a man on the post office wall. The little fellow asked who the man was. "Oh, he's a very bad man," the postmaster told the boy. "He robs banks and steals from mail trains, and the police are trying to catch him so they can put him in jail." The youngster rubbed his chin and then asked, "Why didn't they keep him when they took his picture?"

Sometimes we miss opportunities. Like the reveler who said, "You only live once!" "No," his wise friend intoned, "We live forever, we die once, and a miscarriage there is irretrievable." There are probably more people who will miss God's wonderful banquet due to carelessness than due to perverted evil.

The Power of Punctuation

A woman was traveling through Europe with a friend who tended to be extravagant. Finding a rich tapestry in a quaint shop in Madrid, the spendthrift sent her husband an email as soon as she returned to her hotel room. She went on and on extolling the beauty of the tapestry and mentioning how smashing it would look over the fireplace in their new home. She told him that it was a steal at just $7000 and asked him if she should go ahead and buy it. Her husband, a penny-pinching economist, sent back a terse reply, "No! Cost too high."

Several weeks later the woman returned home and had the tapestry with her. Her husband howled with exasperation. "Didn't you get my email?" he bellowed. "I said, 'No! Cost too high!'" "Oh dear," his wife replied, "I thought you said, 'No cost too high!'"

There are four meaningful observations to consider from this tale: What can be misunderstood will be. Pay careful attention to punctuation when communicating. Spendthrifts tend to think coins are made round to roll; penny-pinchers tend to think they are made flat to stack. In most marriages you will find both.

...Say Something Good

We should make every attempt to live in such a way that we would not be nervous or have any hesitancy selling the family parrot to the town gossip.

We cannot separate character from conduct—we will act out who we are.

Lightweights

It is said that the two most common elements in the universe are hydrogen and stupidity. It seems that the only way some people could be dumber is to weigh more.

Fortunately, God does not call us to be smart, successful, or popular; He calls us to be faithful. That's something that both the brilliant New Yorker and the aborigine hopping around the outback in a loincloth can subscribe to. Solomon proved that. We need a Counselor, one who sticks closer than a brother.

Friend—Or Enemy?

I am your constant companion...I am your greatest helper or your heaviest burden. I will push you onward and upward or drag you down to the gutter. I am at your command. You might just as well turn over half your tasks to me, and I will do them quickly and correctly.

I am easily managed; you must merely be firm with me. Show me exactly how you want something done, and after a few lessons, I will do it automatically. I am the servant of all successful people and alas the master of all failures. Those who are great I have helped to make great, and those who are failures I have made failures.

I am not a machine, but I work with all the precision of a machine, plus the intelligence of a person. You may run me for profit or run me for ruin; it makes no difference to me. Take me, train me, be firm with me, and I will put great treasures at your feet! Be easy with me, and I will destroy you! Who am I? Habit is my name.

Someone once said that today we are made into slaves not by our heredity, but by the habits bred into us in our youth. The achievements of tomorrow are found in the habits formed today!

23

Who's Carrying You?

A very successful man specialized in building fine homes. Nearing the end of his life he requested that all his pallbearers should be bankers. When asked why, he replied, "They've carried me this far, they may as well carry me all the way."

Who's carrying you? If we rely on mere men, we'll fall like an egg from a tall chicken.

Horsin' Around

A man had a picture of a most beautiful young woman. He fell in love with her just through her picture. He discovered that she lived in a distant land. He sold many of his prized possessions in order to purchase an airline ticket and flew to the far off country.

Once there he inquired as to how he might find the beautiful young woman. The local people knew immediately who she was for she was esteemed to be not only the fairest in all the land, but the wisest. They told him he would have to travel many miles into the mountains. After many long hours and near exhaustion, he found the village where she lived. Suddenly, there she was, indescribably radiant. He pursued her for days, showering her with flowers and gifts. But she turned away every advance. After several days and half mad with desire, he loudly proclaimed his love for her in the public square of the village, and said that he must have her as his wife.

Speaking to him for the first time, she said, "If you think that I am beautiful, you should see my sister, and she stands directly behind you." Spinning around, he faced a horse. "What is the meaning of this?" he asked her. "If you were so enchanted with me," the wise young woman replied, "Why were you so quick to turn around?"

What often appears to be true is not always so. Common sense and caution are synonymous with wisdom. One does not rush in where angels are wary to tread.

When Pigs Fly!

A man attending church in the mid-1800s heard the preacher say that one day people would fly through the air like birds. This upset the man so much that he stood to his feet in the middle of the assembly. He proclaimed in a loud voice that other than birds, the only ones who would ever be able to fly were angels. So distraught was he that he determined to leave the church. And so he did, taking his two young sons Wilber and Orville with him.

Most of our limitations are self-imposed. Calcification, or hardening of the categories, sets in about the age of thirty-three. Around this time we begin to see everyone other than us as out of step.

If calcification has gripped your advisors, putty-minded counsel is all you can expect. There is one Counselor who never misses the mark. This is why the Bible is called the Book of Life!

Oops!

The church elders were gathering for their monthly meeting. Barely had they gotten under way when one of them fell out with a heart attack. When the paramedics arrived, they carried out six elders before they found the right one.

Talk about calcification! Most committees are made up of people who individually can do nothing and together decide that nothing can be done!

Get a Job

There was a picturesque town with its quaint shops situated around a charming little square. This town was on a busy road, and many travelers and day-trippers came to enjoy its uniqueness and warm hospitality.

This town was plagued with only one problem. The town reprobate, when not in jail sobering up, lay up against a wheel of the old civil war cannon in the town square, in full view of all the nice clean visitors.

The city council, concerned about the impact this would have on visitors, not to mention the businesses, came up with a plan to rehabilitate the poor wretch of a man, while at the same time, clean up their fair town.

They offered the man a job polishing the cannon. The man took them up on their offer and to everyone's delight, soon had the cannon gleaming. So pleased were the city fathers that they decided to bring the man into the mayor's office and enter into a formal agreement with the man to make him feel real important.

This arrangement continued for several years. One year as they met in the mayor's office, the man said that he had decided not to renew his contract.

Vexed, they asked why. "Don't git me wrong," the man said, "I do appreciate everythin' you folks has done fer me. I've been able to buy me a nice car, even got me a girl who I'm fixin to marry," the man said proudly. "And I've saved me up some money, and I'm gonna buy me my own cannon and go in bidness fer m'self."

Activity without meaning. In the hyper speeds we live at today it's easy to give ourselves to an inferior purpose. The urgent things are seldom important and the important things, like helping to raise the next generation, are seldom urgent.

No Strings Attached?

Two ol' farmers discovered a hole in the ground while working the fields one day. Curious as to how deep the hole was, they threw a stone in and listened for it to hit bottom. Hearing nothing, they pitched in a three foot long piece of 2x4. Still hearing nothing, they found an old railroad tie and pitched it in. Suddenly a pig came charging at them and when he reached them, jumped into the hole.

Several minutes later a neighbor happened by and asked, "Boys, have you seen a pig wanderin' around here anywhere?"

"Sure have neighbor," the men say, "Why just a few minutes ago a pig came stormin' across the field and jumped into this here hole."

"Naw," the man replies, "Couldn't be my pig, mine was tethered to a railroad tie."

While there is some validity to, "He who hesitates is lost," we would probably be well served to make sure that there are no lose strings attached when we take an action.

New Money

I know a businessman who started out poor as a church mouse, but he is now a millionaire. He acquired this sum of money through frugality, conscientious effort to give fair value, perseverance, and the death of an uncle who left him $999,999.50

Poor is nothing if we have everything. Great wealth is nothing if that's all we have.

Goin' to Nashville

There was a young recruit going through basic training who was missing his girl something awful. One night he could take it no longer. Running past the guard at the front gate, he was headed home. The guard called out for him to halt, but the kid kept right on running.

Lifting his rifle to his shoulder the guard yelled, "Halt or I'll fire!"

The kid, never breaking stride, yelled over his shoulder, "My momma's in heaven, my pappy's in hell, my girl's in Nashville, Tennessee, and I'm gonna see one of 'em tonight!"

There's something about that kind of resolve you can't help but admire. But the key question should always be, "Is the trophy worth the chase?"

Think Ahead

The lawyer for an insurance company in a casualty suit was pressing a flashily dressed young woman. Trying to catch her in a contradiction, he asked, "And I'm sure as the elevator fell, all your past sins flashed before your eyes?"

"That's absurd," the woman said, "The elevator only fell nine floors."

While confession is good for the soul, it should always be with forethought.

Like Father...

I have a friend who never made it through college because he kept highlighting his books with black magic markers. He said the happiest school days of his life were the four years he spent in the second grade. They would have passed him on, he said, but they didn't want him to get ahead of his father.

Many of us have failed more tests in life than we've passed, whether in school, life, or our spiritual walk. Thank God he doesn't call us to be smart, successful, or rich; He calls us to be faithful. We can all do that by a decision of the will. Everything in life is a decision. The key is in our "want to's."

The Mercy of God

During the war, American mothers knit thousands of pairs of socks. These acts of kindness were much anticipated by G.I.'s whose feet were often wet and cold.

On one occasion the soldiers barely had time to change their socks when orders came down to move out. One of the young men felt a sharp jab to his heel. Not being able to stop and remove the source of the problem, he limped along in great discomfort until they reached their destination. Pulling off his boot he discovered a small wad of paper. He unrolled it to find this message, "God have mercy on your poor tired feet."

Charles Spurgeon said that the Lord's mercy often rides to the door of our heart upon the black horse of affliction.

In Things Unseen...

Known for their great efficiency, the Germans were launching a magnificent new ocean liner and had invited a high dignitary from Denmark to christen it. On the day of the christening everyone was gathered on the platform, the band was playing, but there was no ship in sight.

As the time drew near for the ceremony to begin, the uneasy Dane asked, "Where's the ship?"

The officiating High German official said, "Never mind da ship, just sving da bottle, da ship vill be dair!"

Faith is the rejection of our senses for the sake of hope. First belief then revelation.

The Truth Can Hurt

A pastor was greeting people as they were leaving church after the service one Sunday when a little girl spoke up as he chatted with her parents. She said to him, "When I grow up, I'm going to give you some money."

The preacher was touched by the girl's good intentions and said, "Well, that's very nice of you, Hermione...why are you going to do that?"

The little girl replied, "'Cause my daddy said, 'That's the poorest preacher I've ever heard!'"

There are two lessons here: Be careful what you say in the presence of others, for your words may come back with teeth attached to them. Secondly, sometimes we learn of our shortcomings in painful ways. But Proverbs says that you have no friend or ally in someone who will not share a truth, and better wounds from a friend than kisses from an enemy.

If He Only Believed...

Russian government apparatchik Mikoyan and Nikita Khruschev were discussing what to do with Joseph Stalin's body when it was removed from Lenin's mausoleum.

"What about sending it to Israel?" Mikoyan suggested.

"Oh no," said Khruschev. "I recall that a long time ago in Israel a man once rose from the dead."

As the contemporary Christian song proclaims, "He's alive and I'm forgiven..."

Stick With What You Know

Georges Courteline, French humorist and satirist, overcame his young adversarial upstart by requesting a duel he knew he couldn't lose.

"My dear sir," he wrote, "As I am the offended party, the choice of weapons is mine. We shall fight with orthography. You, sir, are already dead!"

When we speak, our hearts are revealed and our minds are on parade.

Ready at All Times

A French general and his young American aide, a lieutenant, boarded a train to take them to a high level conference. When they found their compartment and took their seats, they noticed the two women across from them. One was a middle-aged mannerly woman, the other, an ingénue of uncommon beauty.

As they traveled through the bucolic countryside, the train entered a long tunnel. Shortly thereafter, the lights went out casting them into total darkness. Momentarily there was the unmistakable sound of a kiss, followed instantly by the sharp report of a slap.

When the lights came back on, the general sat nonplused with a reddened cheek. He reasoned that the handsome young lieutenant had stolen a kiss from the demure damsel, and because he was seated directly across from her, she mistakenly thought him to be the transgressor, and so, visited upon him her righteous indignation.

The young woman thought that one of them had indeed tried to kiss her, but became disoriented in the darkened car, and the older woman was the recipient of the intrusive affection.

The older woman was positive the general was the

nefarious miscreant and had received his just recompense for his carnal and salacious overstep.

The young American lieutenant thought as the lights went out, "I just can't miss an opportunity like this," kissed the back of his own hand, and slapped the fire out of that French general!

When opportunities arise, we must be ready!

The Tangled Web

A young man and his friend were taking their physicals to be inducted into the Army. Both were not at all excited about looking forward to Army life.

The first young man came out of the exam room all smiles. "Four F," he told his friend. "It's my back brace, the doc said I couldn't get in the Army because of my bad back."

His friend asked if he could borrow the brace. After a quick trip to the restroom he entered the examination room ready to face the doctor. Several minutes later, he emerged crestfallen.

His friend asked him what had happened. "The doc said that anyone who could wear a brace like that upside-down has to be in top physical shape. 'Welcome to the Army, son!'"

> *"Oh what a tangled web we weave*
> *when first we practice to deceive."*
> —*Sir Walter Scott*

The Best Gift of All

There were three brothers, Lud, Lem, and Clem, who decided to do something very special for their mother on her 80th birthday. Lud was the wealthiest of the brothers, and so he had a beautiful home built for her. Lem, who was not quite so well off, purchased a limousine and the services of a chauffeur to transport his dear mother wherever she wanted to go. Clem, the youngest, and his mother's favorite, had limited income so extravagant gifts were beyond his means. He did his best and purchased an exotic parrot for his mother.

The mother thanked the two older sons for their gifts but confided in her youngest son, "Lud's gift of the house is impractical. With my arthritis I can't get around as well as I used to. The house is just too big." About Lem's gift she said, "The limousine is beautiful but stays parked in the garage. With my poor eyesight I couldn't see anything if I did go anywhere." Then she said, "But Clem, you're the only one who gave me something I can use—that little chicken was delicious!"

Gifts don't always have to be expensive or exotic. Sometimes the best gift we can give is ourselves and the willingness to spend time with someone.

Empty the Cup

A man was walking down the street when a woman approached him.

"Help a poor old lady by buying some thread," she pleaded. "I don't sew," the man replied curtly.

"And neither shall ye reap," said the old woman.

"Give and it will be given unto you in full measure, pressed down, shaken together, overflowing," Luke 6:38 tells us. If we empty our cup, God will give us a bigger one.

An Ounce of Prevention...

A young man desperately wanted to win the heart of his lady fair but lacked adroitness in the language of romance. Taking counsel from a wag, he was advised to say, "When I look into your eyes, time stands still."

Time passed and his memory failed him. On the lake under a starry June sky, he looked into the eyes of his beloved and sighed, "You've got a face that would stop a clock."

We need to pay attention to detail; sometimes we need to script and rehearse our presentations.

Bean Counting

As the commuter pulled out of New York headed for Connecticut, the usual crowd gathered in the club car. On and on they went about the business of the day—how stocks had risen or fallen, who made a fortune, and who was reduced to a measly million or two. Over in the corner a small man was talking excitedly about how blacks were steady, while blues and yellows were surprisingly down. Greens and reds, he said, were strong as usual. Finally, one of the tycoons inquired as to what business he might be in. "Jellybeans" the little man said.

Regardless of what's your passion, due your work as unto the Lord, for it is He who has given your hands work to do.

What Was That Again?

The first mate looked forward to one day being the master of the ship. He took note of every move the captain made. One ritual the captain had was most mysterious. Every day he would disappear for several minutes. The first mate decided to follow the captain. He noticed that he went directly to his cabin, locking the door behind him. Taking out a key, he unlocked a drawer in his nightstand, took from it a small book, read something, carefully replaced the book, locked the drawer, and returned to join the others on the bridge.

After many years the captain retired and appointed the first mate as master of the ship. After the captain's departure, the first mate rushed to what was now his stateroom, took out the key which he was now in possession of, and unlocked the drawer in the nightstand. Grasping the little book, he leafed through its pages. The only page that had anything written on it was found in the center of the book. It said, "Left side port, right side starboard."

We need reminding more than we need things new. The Book of Life will not only keep us on an even keel, it will get us to our destination.

Full Steam Ahead!

When Robert Fulton was hard at work on his steam-boat, the people lining the banks said he would never get the thing to float. Then when it went steaming proudly up the Hudson River in 1807, they said he would never get the dern thing to stop. According to them, he could never win.

Most people have a tendency to think in critical, judgmental terms rather than creative, positive ones. They're the ones who never go anywhere.

49

...Speak No Evil...

There was a little six-year-old boy who had never spoken. His parents had taken him to several clinics and had innumerable tests conducted, but to everyone's consternation, no cause could be found.

One day at the dinner table, little Norbert said, "Soup's lousy!" The parents were overcome with joy at discovering that the little fellow could talk. After calming down, they asked their son why he had never said anything. "Up until now," he replied, "everything's been fine."

A fool can ask more questions in seven minutes than a wise man can answer in seven years.

Consequences

A mother told her young son that God would be very upset with his continued refusal to eat his dessert of prunes. Upset over his headstrong refusal to eat it, she ordered him to his room.

Shortly thereafter a fierce thunderstorm struck. Thinking that her son might be frightened by what he imagined to be God's displeasure, she went to his room to console him. She was surprised to find him standing at the window, calmly observing the pelting rain and flashing lightening.

"It's an awful fuss He's making over a few prunes!"

Storms in life are meant for correction or perfection.

One Way

How to get to heaven: Turn right and go straight.

We cannot separate significance from conduct.

Doubtful

A young insurance salesman was out one day looking for a prospect. He took a country road and found the house back in the woods. A creek blocked him from driving up to the house, so he got out of his car and reached the other side by walking on a tree trunk that had fallen across the water. Climbing the steps to the front porch, he knocked on the door. A little old lady with a broom in her hand answered. He asked if she might be interested in buying some insurance. She hated salesmen, so she hit him over the head with the broom and turned her dogs loose on him.

Running for his life, he crossed the creek in one bound and scampered up a tree in order to escape the dogs. After awhile the hounds lost interest and wandered off. The young salesman lowered himself down from the tree and took stock of his condition. A shoe was missing, a sleeve of his jacket was no longer in its rightful place, and he had bruises all over his arms from climbing the tree. Carefully taking his prospecting list from a pocket, he wrote behind her name: "Doubtful."

To be great we must first be good. To be good we must first fail. When you think you're at the end of your rope, you are not at the end of your hope.

Justice Served

An exasperated mother was about to give her young son a well-deserved thrashing when he asked, "Did you ever get a spanking when you were little?" "I most certainly did!" his mother replied. "And did Grandma's mom ever spank her?" "Yes!" the mother said. "And did Great-Grandma's mom spank her?" Softening a little, the mother said, "I assume she did."

The little boy looked at his mother and said firmly, "Don't you think it's about time we stop this hereditary brutality?"

Today, society places a higher value on tolerance than on justice.

Check Ups

A teenage boy was calling perspective customers for his burgeoning lawn mowing business. "Hello," he would begin, "do you need someone to cut your lawn?...Oh, you've got someone?...I'm really good!...Oh, you're very satisfied with who you have now? Well, thank you very much."

After he made several calls like this his mother said, "Now don't get discouraged Billy, just keep persevering, it will come, you'll get some customers."

Billy said, "Oh I'm not looking for more customer's; the people I'm calling are my customers, I'm just checking up on myself!"

Perseverance is good but we also need to check up on ourselves from time to time.

Dead Services

A seven-year-old boy was looking at a plaque in the church foyer listing those killed in service. The pastor noticed that the little boy became more and more upset until he burst into tears. Asking what was troubling him, the little boy asked, "Did all those people die in the eight o'clock service or the ten o'clock service?"

God builds His Church in the hearts of man upon the ruins of legalistic traditions and hollow rituals.

Under Our Noses

Randolph Hearst, publisher and editor of the *San Francisco Examiner*, sent an aide around the world looking for a certain painting he wanted to add to his extensive art collection.

After many weeks the aide returned and reported that the painting was found. It was already a part of the Hearst collection.

Most people concentrate on what they want rather than being satisfied for what they have.

Always on Their Mind

My friend, the late Dr. Norman Vincent Peale, tells about the time he was in Singapore for a speaking engagement. Taking an evening walk, he saw a display board in the window of a tattoo parlor illustrating various images one could have put on their body. He noticed one that was particularly loathsome and entering the parlor to ask the owner who would ever have such a thing put on their body. Without any hesitation the owner said, "Oh, they have that tattooed on their mind long before they ever come in to have it put on their body."

Where we go, what we read, and what we see or look at determines what's tattooed on our mind. What's tattooed on our mind determines what we do. And what we decide to do determines our destiny. Choices not chance dictate our fortunes.

An Uphill Battle

Winston Churchill said that there are only two things more difficult than giving a speech: trying to climb a ladder that's leaning towards you, and kissing a woman who's leaning away from you.

Most things worthwhile are not easily attained. In most cases you know you're on the right path if it's narrow and uphill.

Want No More

A young woman asked her boyfriend if he thought a person with a million dollars experiences more contentment than a person with six children. The boyfriend said the person with six children has more contentment.

"Why do you think so?" she asked. "Because," he replied, "the person with a million dollars always wants more."

Complacency is not always a bad thing!

The Rat Race

The passengers were settled comfortably in their seats when halfway through the flight the pilot came on the intercom and said, "Ladies and gentlemen, I have some disturbing news and some good news. The disturbing news is that the plane's compass has malfunctioned and we're not quite sure where we are. The good news is that we are enjoying a strong tail wind and are making excellent time."

And so it is with many of us, running in the rat race to who knows where.

Pie in the Face

A man and his wife, who had stopped by his office, were entering the elevator when a pretty young secretary got on at the last second.

Poking a finger in the man's ribs, she cooed, "Hello, sweetie pie!"

Without so much as a ruffle, the wife leaned over and said, "Hello, I'm Mrs. Pie."

To act and not over-react is an admirable trait.

Holding the Chicken

A maiden was walking along one bright and beautiful day when she encountered a handsome young man carrying a watermelon under one arm and a chicken under the other arm. In his left hand he carried a washtub, and in his right, a fox.

The man called out a greeting to the lovely maiden, "Good morning fairest of all maidens," he said.

"I dare not speak to thee," the maiden rejoined.

"Why not?" the handsome young man prevailed.

"Because you might try to kiss me," she said.

He replied, "But how could that be, for as you can plainly see, my hands and arms are fully engaged."

"Well," the maiden said demurely, "you could put the fox under the washtub, and you could put the watermelon on top of the washtub to keep the fox from escaping, and I could hold your chicken."

A man pursues a woman until she catches him.

Danger...Danger...

One day a man known for abusing the privilege of being stupid, decided to race a train to the crossing. He lost and hit the forty-third car.

Sometimes we stubbornly refuse to acknowledge the signs of danger that keep flashing before our eyes.

Genuine Fakes

Where did you meet that beautiful woman you're squiring these days?" a man asked his wealthy friend.

"I dunno," the friend answered, "I opened my wallet and there she was."

The wealthier we become, the more discerning we have to be about genuine friendships.

Which Are You?

"What's the difference between being beautiful or charming?" the young woman asked her mother.

"Well," replied her wise mother, "A beautiful woman is one men take notice of, while a charming woman is one who takes notice of a man."

It's Greek to Me

A professor of Greek tore his suit and took it to a tailor by the name of Parthenian from Athens. Mr. Parthenian examined the suit, and asked, "Euripides?" "Yes," said the professor. "Eumenides?"

If you want to communicate more effectively, especially if you're in sales, it's important to get on the same level with the other person. Whether prospecting or evangelizing, meet the other person where they're at.

Chomping at the Bite

The doctor asked the wife of a very rotund fellow, "Does your husband eat between meals?"

"My husband has no between meals," the wife answered.

The good man eats to live, while the evil man lives to eat (Prov. 13:25 Liv. Bible).

Thanks, But No Thanks!

A husband drew up his chair beside his wife while she was doing some work on her sewing machine. "Don't you think you're running too fast?" he asked. "Look out! You'll sew the wrong seams. Slow down, watch your fingers! Steady!"

"What on earth is the matter with you?" his wife asked with alarm. "I've been using this machine for years."

"Well, dear, I thought you might like me to help you, since you are always helping me when I'm driving the car."

Illustrations can often be effective when mere words fail.

A Petite Perspective

A most confident woman had a massive girth. One day the doctor asked her what size dress she wore. She confidently replied, "52—petite."

People with low self esteem will more often than not, base their self-worth on whom they know, what they can do, or what they own.

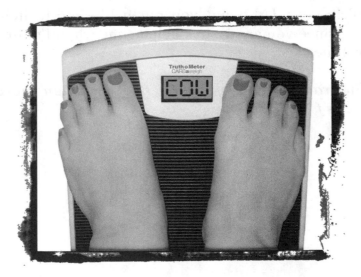

Show Business

One Sunday morning the pastor of a large church entered the pulpit and warbled in a singsong manner, "My name is Michael Dugan, I am the senior pastor here at St. Anthony's church, my salary is $40,000 a year and I'm in deep need of a raise in salary."

No sooner had he taken his seat than the associate pastor stood to his feet and began in the same manner, "My name is Bill Masters, I am the associate pastor here at St. Anthony's church, my salary is $35,000 a year, and I too am in desperate need of a raise in salary."

Barely had he finished when the music minister chimed in. "My name is Tommy Bates, I'm the organist here at St. Anthony's church, my salary is $52,000 a year and...THERE'S NO BUSINESS LIKE SHOW BUSINESS LIKE NO BUSINESS I KNOW!

In music city – Nashville, Tennessee – pastors of many churches refer to their people not as congregations but as audiences.

71

Where Are You?

A party of hunters hired one of their group's brothers, a guide familiar with the northeast, to take them into the backwoods of Maine. Several days later the hunters realized that they were totally lost.

They complained to their guide, "You told us you were the best guide in Maine."

"It's true," the guide answered, "but I believe we are now in Canada."

If you are in this world but not of this world, it is critically important to listen to a guide that sticks closer than a brother.

Sticking Like Glue

The wife asked her husband if he would still love her when her hair was gray.

"Why, haven't I stuck with you through brunette, red, blond, and Tennessee Titans blue?" he asked.

There is one who speaks rashly, but the tongue of the wise brings healing (Prov. 12:18 New American Standard).

How Long?

One woman was complaining to her rival that she had been at the beauty salon for four hours.

"It's terrible," said her nemesis, "that you had to wait all that time and then not get waited on."

Some people get their kicks by stepping on other's dreams.

The Ball That Blinds

Bob Feller of the Cleveland Indians was facing what he hoped would be his last batter during the second game of a double-header against the old Washington Senators. Cleveland had handily won the first game and was leading in the second. A rookie was at bat for Washington; it was the bottom of the ninth, two outs, and the count was three and two. One more strike and Feller could enjoy a nice refreshing shower.

Rollie Hemsley, the catcher for Cleveland, and an inveterate practical joker, came out to the mound to confer with Feller. Hemsley wanted Feller to throw an imaginary pitch to the kid and see if they could fool him. Feller, sweaty and tired, resisted. Hemsley persisted until Feller finally agreed. Feller, who could fire a blinding fastball, wound up and threw a pitch but kept the ball tucked into his glove. Hemsley smacked his glove with his fist and waited for the call. Instantly the umpire stood straight up and thundered, "Steee...rike three!"

The rookie got up out of his batter's stance, looked at the ump and said, "I thought that was a ball myself!"

You can fool some of the people all of the time, and all of the people some of the time, but you can't fool all of the people all of the time.

The Real Thing

Once Charlie Chaplin, who delighted millions with his on screen antics as the Little Tramp, was on an unpublicized vacation in Monaco for some well-deserved rest and relaxation. Looking out his hotel window he noticed that a nearby theater was to hold a Charlie Chaplin look-alike contest the next evening.

On a lark Chaplin decided to enter the contest. Putting on his mustache, his funny oversized shoes, derby, and grabbing his cane, he was off to the theater. He entered the contest and came in third.

Life is full of pretenders and imitators. Knowing the genuine article is critical in all areas of our lives.

The Taste of Chicken

The youngest boy in a family of eight brothers was fifteen years old before he learned that there was more to a chicken than gravy.

You snooze—you lose.

Major in Minors

A young lady was taking golfing lessons from the club pro in order to eliminate a mean slice. Everything was proceeding nicely until she sliced a drive that went over some trees and hit a passing motorist who then sideswiped a bus, sending it into a ravine where it overturned.

Horrified over the mayhem caused by her errant ball, she turned to the instructor and pled, "Oh, what shall I do?"

Ever the consummate pro, the instructor replied, "I think if you bring your hand a little more over the club…"

Most of us are more in need of minor corrections than major changes.

Come Again?

A man in the hospital was being reassured by his boss, "Now don't you worry about things at the office, we've all agreed to pitch in and help complete your work—as soon as we can figure out just exactly what it is that you do."

Positive expectations are never a substitute for doing the difficult work.

Wrong on Both Counts

The daughter told her mother that she could not marry her suitor. "Why?' the mother wanted to know, "he seems like a very nice young man."

"For two reasons," said the daughter, "he says he's a confirmed atheist and doesn't believe in hell."

"Oh, never mind that," said the mother, "go ahead and marry him, between the two of us we'll convince him he's wrong."

God sends people into our lives to bless us or afflict us according to our needs. As iron sharpens iron, so one person sharpens another.

The Revolving Door

It used to be that a mother would save her wedding dress for her daughter to wear at her wedding; today, the daughter saves her wedding dress for her next wedding. Some get married so often they need a wash-and-wear wedding gown!

Totally Prepared

A smart young woman said that when she marries she's going to marry a career soldier.

"Why's that?" asked a friend.

"Because they can sew, cook, make the bed, are in good health, and are used to taking orders," the hopeful young woman replied.

The Ups and Downs of Life

A man was responding to an inquiry by his insurance company requesting more details regarding a job related injury. The man wrote back.

"Please find detailed explanation in box three. Another worker and myself were hoisting a barrel of bricks to the top floor of a new office building. The bucket was near the top when my partner got a sneezing attack and let go of the rope. For some reason I did not let go of the rope. The barrel of bricks weighed 250 lbs. I weigh 135lbs.

"About the sixth floor I met the barrel coming down. This will explain how I got the broken collarbone and severe lacerations about my head and shoulders. When I reached the top, my fingers jammed into the pulley. This is how I sustained my broken fingers and hand. As I freed my fingers from the pulley, the barrel hit the ground with such force that the bottom came out of the barrel.

"Because my weight was now greater than the empty barrel, I found myself quickly on the descent. Around the sixth floor I again encountered the barrel. This will explain the three broken ribs. I landed on the bricks and broke my right leg. This time, however, I had the presence of mind to let go of the rope.

"The barrel came flying back down and landed on me as I lay in agony on the bricks. It broke my right leg in a second place, and I sustained multiple internal injuries. Sincerely yours."

Have you ever had days where you felt like you kept getting hit by the barrel?

2 Corinthians 4:7 says, "We are hard pressed on every side, but not crushed; perplexed, but not in despair; persecuted, but not abandoned; struck down, but not destroyed."

A Place for Us

Some people must think that Sunday worship service is like a convention—many families only send one delegate!

And sadly, that member may interpret regular attendance as every Easter.

Light Your Fire!

One of Billy Graham's favorite stories is about a fire that broke out in a small town church. When the firefighters arrived, the pastor recognized one of them.

"Hello there, Mike, I haven't seen you in church for a long time," he chided.

"Well," answered the sweating man wrestling a fire hose, "there hasn't been a fire in church for a long time."

The Pharisees had the art of worship. King David had the heart of worship.

Ashes to Ashes

A pastor was visiting one of his members who had become most lax about attendance. The man had proclaimed that he could find God on the Sabbath just as well out on the lake fishing as he could in church. They sat in silence before the open fireplace, the man knowing the pastor had come to take him to task; the preacher knowing he was expected to give a deserved rebuke.

After a long period of silence, the pastor arose from his chair and went to the fireplace. Taking the tongs, he lifted a single coal from the embers and placed it alone on the hearth. Saying nothing he waited while the coal quickly burned to a black ash as the nearby fire blazed on.

"You don't have to say anything," the man said, "I know what you mean. I cannot keep the fire of faith burning alone. I'll be in my place at church next Sunday."

Divide to conquer and isolation are two strategies the devil uses to defeat us.

Same Ol' Same Ol'

A young boy said, "Our minister preaches the same sermon every Sunday—he just yells in different places."

Repetition is the mother of study, but variety and amiability help palatability.

A Pig in a Poke

A young minister from New York accepted a pastorate in the Ozark Mountains. After he settled in, he joined one of the local civic clubs and was told that new members had to serve a term as "hog caller."

The young minister protested that he felt such a title was not in keeping with "a man of the cloth." His fellow club member's nevertheless insisted that he take his turn in the office.

Reluctantly agreeing, he said, "Well, I will serve as hog caller. I came here to be the shepherd of the flock—but you know your people better than I."

Someone once asked Charles Wesley if he didn't have to subject himself to insufferable indignities as he spread the Gospel message. "No more indignities than the average politician running for political office," was Wesley's reply.

Creature of Habit

There was a preacher who only used two gestures in all of his sermons. One gesture was up, and the other was down, and the second always followed the first.

One fine Sunday morning he was expounding with great exuberance and said, with his hand held high, pointing towards the heavens, "When the roll is called up yonder"...then pointing downward with a majestic sweep of his arm, he shouted "...I'll be there!"

As anyone who has witnessed one motorist offering another a half-a-piece sign, gestures can lead to unintended conclusions.

Back in the Woods...

A backwoods preacher was discussing sin with a pipe-smoking hill woman who was a member of his church.

She said, "Parson, you are a fine preacher for us hill folks. We never really knowed what sin was until you come here."

What can be misunderstood probably will be.

A Sweet Deal

The following is a letter from a farm kid at Marine boot camp training on Parris Island:

Dear Ma an' Pa,

This joinin' the Marines is the best dern thing I ever done. Tell Vernon and Buford they'd better hurry an' join up befer all the places is filled.

I can sleep in 'til 6 a.m. and all ya do when ya git up is smooth out yer cot an' shine a couple things...no cows ta milk, chickens ta feed, no hogs ta slop, or wood ta split...Nothin! Well, men gotta shave, but heck, thar's warm water.

Breakfast is with all the trimmins: juices, aggs, bacon, and cereal, ifn's ya want. They's a little light on steak, ham, tater's, an' grits. They's two city boys who seem ta live on coffee, so's I git their food lots a times. That keeps me 'til noon when they feed ya agin.

We go on what the Sergeant calls "route" marches...haint no further than to our mail box, but the city boys get sore feet an' we all ride back in trucks.

Vernon an' Buford u'll git a kick otta this'n. They've

done give me a heapa medals fer shootin' at a bulls-eye that's big as a chipmunk's head...and it don't move none. And, it don't shoot back attcha like the Clayton's do thar at home.

We practice that thar hand-ta-hand combat fightin.' Ya git to wrestle with them city boys. Ya got's ta be real careful though cause they break easy. Shucks, after fightin' that ol' bull at home, this ain't nothing! Fact tis, I'm 'bout the best they got, exceptins for old "Tank" Hawkins from over in Zeller's holler. He joined same time I done. But I'm only 5' 6" an' 130 lbs. He's 6' 5" an weighs near 250 dry!

Be sure an' tell Vernon an' Buford ta hurry on now befer others find out 'bout this here deal an' come a stampedin' in here.

Your lovin' daughter,

Mabelene

Never, ever, underestimate the power of a woman!

Doing the Impossible

A salute to secretaries and administrative assistants:

We, the willing, led by the unknowing, are doing the impossible for the ungrateful. We have done so much with so little for so long that we are now qualified to do anything with nothing!

These people are the most under-appreciated and underpaid employees in the American workforce.

The Impossible (Part Two)

PERSONNEL DIRECTOR: "What previous experience have you had and what kind of work have you done?"

APPLICANT: "I was an administrative assistant. All I had to do was look like a girl, think like a man, act like a lady, and work like a dog."

If secretaries and administrative assistants were paid based on what they do, most companies couldn't afford very many of them.

A Widow's Dream

A pastor took up a collection for a special cause, telling his congregation that whoever gave the most could pick out a special hymn the following Sunday. When the money was counted, the pastor was delighted to find that the dear, soft-spoken widow, Mrs. Jones, had contributed a thousand dollars.

The next Sunday the pastor, with her permission, brought her forward to honor her for her kind generosity. The pastor, true to his word, asked her what favorite hymn she would like to select.

Her eyes brightened as she looked out over the congregation. Pointing to the most handsome available bachelor in the building she said, "I'll take him!"

Some people just know what they're after.

Fraidy Cats

I knew a kid in school that was so modest he couldn't bring himself to write an improper fraction on the blackboard.

His dad was the same way; he didn't have enough courage to second a motion. In fact, he couldn't even lead a group in silent prayer!

Caught Unawares...

As we all know, parrots can be well trained. A man bought a parrot at an auction after a time of spirited bidding.

As he was paying for the bird he asked the auctioneer if the bird could talk. "Talk?" the auctioneer replied, "he's been bidding against you for the last thirty minutes."

Some people are born unlucky and have a relapse.

Man's Best Friend

A man entered a movie theater while the feature was in progress and took a seat. When his eyes acclimated to the darkness, he was surprised to discover that a dog occupied the seat next to him. He then became aware that the dog's owner was in the next seat beyond the dog. The man was fascinated by the keen interest the dog took in the movie. When there was something sad or moving the dog responded with soft whimpering; with each amusing incident, the dog yipped with glee.

After the movie when the house lights came up, the man commented to the dog's owner how amazed he was over the dog's interest in the picture. The owner said, "This was a surprise to me too, he didn't care a thing for the book."

Never Satisfied

A shopping center for husbands was opened recently where a woman could go to choose a mate. This shopping center had five floors of available bachelors, each floor as you ascended contained men of increasingly positive attributes. There was only one restriction—once you opened the door at any level, you could not go back down other than to leave the building.

Some girlfriends decided to try it out. The first floor had a sign by the door saying, "These men have good jobs and love kids." *This is good* they thought, but curiosity drove them to the second floor.

The sign next to the door on this floor read, "These men have high paying jobs, love kids, and are very handsome." "Hmmm," the girls said, "but what might floor three hold?"

They reached the third floor to find a sign that stated: "These men have high paying jobs, love kids, are very, very good looking, and help around the house." "Wow!" the women exclaimed, "Very tempting! But there's more further up." So up they go.

The sign on the fourth level read, "These men have extremely high paying jobs, love kids, are the crème de la crème of good looking men in America, help out around the house, and have strong romantic tendencies." "Oh, mercy us," they cried, "but can you only imagine what must be waiting for us on floor five?" They crammed onto the express elevator and stampeded off at the fifth floor. This sign read, "This floor is just to prove that some people are impossible to please. Thank you for shopping with us and have a pleasant day."

What the eye admires, the heart desires. It's an admirable quality to be able to keep from overreaching.

Handwriting on the Wall...

A church was so uncertain about their pastor that when he entered the hospital for an operation, the Board of Trustees called a special meeting to vote on whether they should send a get-well card.

Unfortunately for the sick man, the vote was eight to four—against!

Here and There

Headlines from around the country:

Police Begin Campaign to Run Down Jaywalkers

Teacher Strikes Idle Kids

Cold Wave Linked to Temperatures

Red Tape Holds Up New Bridges

New Study of Obesity Looks for Larger Test Group

Local High School Dropouts Cut in Half

Hospitals Are Sued by 7 Foot Doctors

Typhoon Rips Through Cemetery; Hundreds Dead

Iraqi Head Seeks Arms

Wired for the Truth

Police in Radnor, Pennsylvania, interrogating a not-too-bright suspect, placed a metal colander on his head and connected it to a photocopy machine with wires. The message "He's lying" was placed in the copier and each time the police believed the suspect wasn't telling the truth, they pressed the print button.

Seeing the message "He's lying" repeatedly coming out of what he perceived to be a "lie detector," the suspect confessed.

You can fool all the people some of the time, and some of the people all the time.

The New Math

A man entering a fast food restaurant ordered a half dozen chicken wings to go. The young person behind the counter pointed to a sign saying you could order 6, 9, or 12 chicken wings. The man said, "Well, give me a half dozen."

"We don't have a half dozen chicken wings," the youngster patiently said, "we only have six, nine, or twelve."

"So, I can't order a half dozen, but I can order six?" the man asked.

"Now you've got it," replied the relieved young person behind the counter.

Some people will die terminally silly.

Clueless

A person was in the process of checking out at a grocery store and placed one of those rubber dividers between their things and the person's things behind them.

The check out clerk rang up all the items and then picked up the divider. Looking for a bar code and finding none, she asked if the person knew how much it was.

"I think I've changed my mind about that, I don't think I'll get that today."

The clerk never blinked, and set the bar aside, having no idea what had just happened.

The quintessential example of non compus mentis.

Hot Question

A computer troubleshooter was busy processing data one evening at the central office of a large metropolitan bank. Suddenly the phone rang.

The woman on the other end of the line was calling from one of the bank's branch offices and inquired, "There's smoke coming out of the back of my computer. Do you have a fire downtown?"

This person disproved the old adage, "Where there's smoke, there's fire."

Finding One's Purpose

A half dozen pre-schoolers were being delivered home one day when a fire truck flew by, sirens blaring. Seated proudly atop the big rig was a Dalmatian. This started a discussion among the children as to what the dog's purpose was.

One youngster said he believed the dog was meant to keep the crowds at a safe distance from the fire. Another disagreed, saying he thought the dog was for good luck.

A smart little girl brought the conversation to a close by saying that the firemen used the dog to find the fire hydrant.

Out of the mouths of babes...

The Better Way

A man visiting a city on business developed a severe toothache. Seeking relief from his distress he looked in the phone book for a dentist. Finding one that had an opening, he made his way to the good doctor's office.

After a preliminary examination and x-ray, the dentist informed the man that the tooth needed to come out.

"How much?" the man inquired.

"One hundred dollars," the dentist replied.

"Why, that's pretty high, it won't take but just a minute," the man complained.

"Oh, I can do it more slowly if you like," the dentist offered.

We should never confuse the skill it takes to do a task with the time in which it takes to do it.

A Biblical Role

A man and his wife fell into a dispute over who should prepare the coffee in the mornings. The man argued that she should do it because she was in charge of all the preparation of food and beverages.

She objected, saying that it would not only be a nice gesture if he would do it, but that it was biblical.

"I can't believe that," the husband responded, "show me."

So she brought forth the family Bible, opened it to the New Testament and showed him where it clearly said at the top of several pages... "HEBREWS."

You just can't beat a woman's logic!

Nuts!

A lady approached a showcase displaying a great variety of nuts from all over the world.

"Who handles the nuts?" the woman asked somewhat imperiously.

The young wag behind the counter responded, "Please be patient ma'am, I'll wait on you in just a minute."

Bouncing Back

Have you heard about the boat on its way to America from Taiwan with a load of yo-yo's? It ran into high seas and sank...a hundred and forty-seven times!

And isn't that how we feel when faced with trials and tribulations. One day we're up, the next day we're down. We need a pilot in the storms of life.

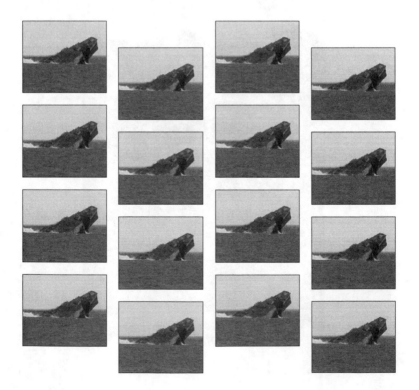

Wrong Lesson Learned

A mother kept trying to reinforce in her young son that he should treat his sister as a treasure. One day she caught him striking his sister.

She scolded him saying, "What have I told you about how to treat your sister? Tell me!"

The boy, obviously influenced by stories and cartoons about pirates and sunken treasures, said, "To bury her and dig her up?"

It's important not to assume that the other person knows the meaning of the words we use.

What's in a Name?

In the late 1800s two lawyers in New York agreed to form a partnership. Israel Ketchum and Uriah Cheatham became well known throughout the area as, I. Ketchum and U. Cheatham.

A man by the name of Abel Crook was once a prominent lawyer in New York City.

Dilly, Daly, Doolittle, and Stahl was the actual name of a law firm in Akron, Ohio.

Argue and Phibbs practiced law together in Ireland.

Wind and Wind practiced law in Chicago, known as the "windy city."

Trivial Pursuits

People wouldn't get divorced for such trivial reasons if they didn't get married for such trivial reasons.

Enough said.

Famous Last Words

Here are a few famous last words:

*"Gimme a match,
I think my gas tank is empty."*

"Let's see if this gun's loaded."

*"You can make it;
that train isn't coming very fast."*

"Watch me do a swan dive
from this bridge."

*"What, your mother's going to
stay another month!"*

"Gosh, woman, these biscuits are tough."

For John Grogan's speaking availability,
please write:

John Grogan International
49 Chandler-Radford Rd.
Mt. Juliet, TN 37122-3444